CARL CARADO

Loving Yourself and Finding Joy

A 10-Step Practical Guide for the New You

First edition

This book was professionally typeset on Reedsy.
Find out more at reedsy.com

To those who made me believe that possibilities exist in all of us.

If you look at what you have in life, you'll always have more. If you look at what you don't have in life, you'll never have enough.

-Oprah Winfrey

Contents

Foreword

The process of loving yourself is uniquely yours. Sometimes, it is almost impossible to imagine what life could have been like if our situations today were different. But thinking about the past may rekindle bursts of clarity, happiness, and joy. This goes to show that we are all capable of experiencing greatness. While life has thrown many challenges, we must never forget that while we continue living, we'll always have the opportunity to reclaim greatness and continue our journey of life and establish our rightful place in this world. So, when we seek clarity and wisdom, we need to sustain our love for ourselves by maintaining our overall well-being and finding our passions. Only then can we keep igniting the spark that fires our souls.

Acknowledgement

To my mother, who continues to inspire me even in her physical absence.
To my husband, who makes me believe that love conquers all each day.

One

Introduction

We see it every day and hear it everywhere. People are living the dream, at least on the surface. Success is defined differently for all of us; successful people live their best lives and are not shy to flaunt it. They don't necessarily work harder, but they sure make it a point to live a life they love and do the things that bring them happiness. And you might say to yourself, why not me? But, if this is a question that you are still asking, then it's time to figure out how to identify that passion, spark the fire, and enjoy the things that you are doing.

It's time to change your life if you feel bored with it or are not accomplishing the things you should be. You might be prevented from achieving the goals you've set for your life by challenges or concerns. The time has come to overcome the obstacles and realize your dreams.

Many people need clarification about their passion. They want to work toward success because they see so many other people doing it, but they need to figure out how. You might need to know that the thing you love is before you. It is possible to make money from any passion.

But, to make it happen, you must recognize the approach you must follow.

So, despite your belief that you can't support yourself financially, you shouldn't resist doing it. Finding your true passion is what this book is all about. You will pick up ideas that are not necessarily groundbreaking but may be underutilized or forgotten, enabling you to identify what gives your life a spark. Therefore, you can follow your passion and turn it into action.

After reading this book, you'll have a basic road map of who you are because you were inspired to ask questions about things that drive you. Then, by following your passion and taking action, you will understand what must be done to begin working on achieving your dreams.

Two

Deciding to be Happy

It is your decision whether to be unhappy. In terms of your life and the choices you make, you are entirely in charge. People assess happiness using many different metrics. For example, some individuals believe that having money will make them happy. Still, they may be dissatisfied due to the everyday tasks they must perform to earn money.

You may aspire to be like others who have everything. These factors could be your financial situation, assets, social standing, or job title. But unfortunately, happiness is not always the result of these things.

Happiness is a Choice

Many people endure unhappy lives even when they are wealthy and in high positions. These people might work in career tracks they dread to the point of hatred, yet all they have is a knack for making money. On the contrary, people who have less, are alone, widowed, etc., exude genuine happiness. Happiness starts inside. While there can be various reasons to resist the temptation to be happy, it's a feeling that we all desire and, hopefully, sustain. Happiness is not about instant gratification, or it is for some. Still, only you can say whether you are genuinely happy.

Philosophers, theologians, psychologists, and even economists have made long-standing efforts to define it. Positive psychology, a distinct subfield of psychology, has been working to identify it since the 1990s. Living a whole life is a critical component of happiness, a state of well-being with a sense of meaning and profound contentment. It is more than just a feeling of good cheer. It's exciting and challenging to achieve happiness.

Natural Joy or Happiness?

Although they are both beautiful emotions to feel, joy and happiness are very different. Joy is cultivated internally and is more consistent. Happiness is typically externally triggered and dependent on other people, things, places, thoughts, and events. Joy is something that everyone strives to achieve. Acceptance comes when you come to terms with who you are, why, and how.

Happiness is said to depend on circumstances outside of yourself. The Dalai Lama noted happy emotions are frequently "like a butterfly that lands on us and then flutters away." However, researchers have discovered that people from all over the world rank happiness higher than other desirable personal outcomes like completing wealth, acquiring material goods, and even entering heaven.

Some people indeed have a pleasant disposition by nature. A genetic predisposition may provide evidence for this. However, if you lack a tendency toward happiness, this does not imply that you were born to be miserable. Your DNA may impact your satisfaction, but this is not a set factor.

If you are not naturally cheerful, you can alter your thoughts and feelings to become one. The idea is to transform how your brain processes information and how you behave. You can accomplish this by developing daily habits that will increase your happiness, which will teach you to genuinely smile more and be a happier person because you flipped a switch internally.

Happiness is Subjective

In life, some random things might bring you joy. Because happiness is a personal experience, they are arbitrary. For example, with rides like roller coasters and bungee jumping, you might experience excitement and happiness. However, this exhilaration might be worse and torment someone terrified of heights. Therefore, they would never attempt a roller coaster or jump from a bridge supported by bungee cords. Happiness is really what we call it, and everyone strives to be happy in their unique manner.

You deserve to pursue your natural high because it makes you feel exhilarated or on cloud 9. What brings you happiness should carry no guilt feelings but only delight and pride. Even if it may seem subjective, what you exude externally is noticeable and may even be unforgettable to others.

It's not a secret that there are health benefits to experiencing happiness. A growing body of research shows that joy positively impacts your physical well-being. Positive emotions and fulfillment have long-term stabilizing effects on blood pressure, inflammation levels, the immune system, cardiovascular health, and other organ systems. In addition, even longer life expectancy and better health and well-being have been associated with happiness.

Separately, a thing that we may take for granted is the power of hugs. Our skin is the largest organ, and as such, it gathers so much data from the outside world. Hugging someone sends these signals to the brain that raises the hormone, Oxytocin, a happy hormone sometimes called the "love hormone." So, give hugging more time, whether you're with someone or even if it's your pet. A warm hug warms the heart.

Rest and Sleep

A major component of happiness is getting enough sleep. Loving yourself requires that you be able to function efficiently. Lack of sleep can make you irritable, unable to think effectively, and highly miserable. There are scientific studies on the impact of sleep adequacy on regenerating body tissues. However, consistently getting quality rest and not just the number of hours with your eyes closed is a game changer.

Even though you may only receive a few hours of sleep, it might be enough to make you feel rested. On the other hand, you may be sleeping too much or possibly not sleeping correctly. While some people need a firm cushion, others want a particularly fluffy pillow to sleep well. Lack of sleep could also be influenced by your physical surroundings, sounds from your partner, squeaky bed, and countless other reasons. Your health can suffer from not getting enough sleep.

A healthy diet is also required to ensure total well-being. If you don't feel good physically, it affects how you function and, eventually, your ability to rest. There are new headlines about what you should or shouldn't eat daily. Studies frequently share groundbreaking (or so it seems) information on how particular foods may benefit or harm us. Fad diets come and go. There are constantly new products on the market that promise rapid weight loss. Not to mention any advice you might receive from influential people, friends, and family. It might seem overwhelming and perplexing.

It's more complex than one might think to define what a healthy diet should consist of today. But you know your body, and you can't continue to be ignorant of facts. Now is the time to learn about it little by little. But using common sense, it ought to contain a variety of foods from various food groups. In addition, it should provide the vitamins and minerals you require and enough calories to keep you at a healthy weight. However, a proper diet is only one component of the solution. Finally, timing is everything to get enough rest and sleep. Time goes faster when you're busy, and sadly for many of us, this cuts into our rest time.

Your inability to sleep could be the root cause of your misery. It could imply a variety of reasons if you have trouble falling asleep and lie up all night long staring at the alarm. Some individuals struggle to fall asleep because of extreme depression and other reasons. Getting a good night's sleep is necessary for happiness. If you're unsure of the root cause, it may be time to consult a professional. It's perfectly the right thing to do. Start with your physician, be honest, be prepared to listen, and be open to recommendations.

Physical Activities

We can never take for granted the value of physical activity helps the brain release hormones, which are responsible for making you feel good, and are incredibly beneficial to the body. For overall health, exercise is crucial. I am not saying that you engage in a strenuous fitness regimen daily. However, it would be best if you attempted to exercise every day. You can receive an incredible amount of exercise by simply completing home chores and cleaning the house. The goal of this is not mainly to lose weight. It has to do with fostering joy while doing it that makes you happy. Complement it with listening to music or even humming to your favorite tune. The bottom line is, having the ability to do so is already a gift—a reason to be grateful.

Relaxing the Mind

Meditating doesn't imply that you are a cult member or engaging in ungodly religious behavior. But unfortunately, many believe that meditation is incorrect because they relate to a religion they are neither affiliated with nor believe in. Meditation is one of the best ways to alter subjective well-being. Doctors have established that meditation causes left-side brain activation, producing a happy emotion in the body. Meditation can be anything that centers, quiets your mind, or allows you to breathe refreshingly.

You might believe that meditation and prayer are identical. Because both require you to shut your eyes, be alone, and concentrate on your thoughts. But each practice has its unique advantages and distinctions. For example, prayer among religious people is well known. They consider prayer a channel for communicating with God and offering Him praise. Some people pray to feel connected to God and to give God their energy.

Prayers are common in most religions, ranging from asking for forgiveness to healing the sick. At the same time, prayers with similar purposes exist in Christianity and Judaism. Islam, for instance, mandates five times a day of prayer intending to thank Allah; Christian and Jewish prayers also have similar intentions.

A prayer is a tool used by religious people to develop a stronger relationship with God. On the other hand, connecting with a higher power is not a part of meditation. Instead, the objective is for you to establish a relationship with yourself. Therefore, you focus your energy inward, focus on your breathing, and sit in silence rather than utter your thoughts aloud. The practice of meditation is entirely personal and aids in achieving a state of spiritual clarity but has no connection with a higher power or deity. So, if prayer achieves the same effect of calming the mind and body, practice it often.

There are so many meditative techniques available out there. Let's try one. Sit comfortably, hands on your thighs, your back is straight, and your chin leveled. Now close your eyes, take 3 seconds to inhale, hold your breath for 3 seconds, and release for 4 seconds. Repeat five times. It wasn't that hard, right? But think of what you have done in that short period. You were able to allow your mind to rest, thus making your body relax. Notice the difference? Try to do this when you've been on the go for a long time throughout your day.

Three

Reflections

You need to ask yourself many questions when you're seeking your genuine passion because you want to be happy in life or there's a void you need to fill. This is a challenging task for some, but it is also possible. However, this is a necessary step. The journey to loving yourself requires processing the things that got you to where you are today and figuring out where you'd like to see yourself going.

By thoughtfully answering these questions, you can learn more about yourself and what prevents you from pursuing your activities or a career and living a happy life. Here are several self-reflective questions you ought to ask yourself. Consider taking out a notepad or making a mental note to answer these questions. Typically, it is advisable to write down the responses.

What sparks the fire in you?

The answer to this question might be tricky, but if you've answered other similar questions before, you might find it. You must, however, be highly explicit about your sources of inspiration. What kinds of things do you find interesting and exciting? There is no reason to overthink this. This week, think about one thing you did that gave you a lasting feeling of goodness. Sometimes, our answers are in front of us or near us. We must be patient, pause, be silent, and listen to that whisper that tells us to trust our gut and go with it.

If your life is failure-proof, what would you do?

Due to past failures or fear of failure, many people refrain from taking risks. Yet, what would you do without a doubt if you knew there was no chance you would fail? Failures are opportunities that you can use in the future. Therefore, taking a leap of faith is necessary to get us to our next pit stop.

Remember that life is a marathon, and you need to develop the stamina to sustain yourself. Experiencing obstacles can help you become more resilient, aware of red flags, and bound not to repeat actions that did not work. Every hill you climb and every step you've taken carries nuggets of lessons, bits of inspiration, and motivational snacks that you can take until you get to your next destination.

What would you do if you had to start from scratch again?

Many people are in predicaments where they would like to do better. They do their jobs and go to work because they must, not because they look forward to it. If you had a chance to start again and choose a different path, would you seize the chance to do so, or would you prefer to stay where you are? What would you do? These are not necessarily about regrets, but what are your takeaways in your moments of clarity from a specific experience? Some call this a debrief, which could be a debrief of your life. Start with things that you believe can get you to your quick wins. Successes that will fill your cup so you can move on and take the next step. In my experience, the longer I contemplate, the harder it becomes to jumpstart anything.

If financial resources were not a problem, what would you do?

Many people aspire to become what they would like to realize. Still, financial resources are always a factor for many to be able to do so. So, consider what you would do with the money if you had it. I caution you to think about things that will sustain your internal joy. The hope is for this sustenance to last you a lifetime. Something that gives you that extra smile every day and which you look forward to doing or experiencing because it never gets old. Everything is possible here.

What is your biggest dream?

What is your biggest dream, if any? This is a loaded question and one of the most challenging things to answer in life. Sometimes I wonder if there is even that one thing. We evolve as human beings, and our childhood dreams may change over time. But for this exercise, ideally, it would be best if you had a plan or goal you wanted to achieve.

What does your situation look like concerning your dream? Do you want to attend college but are a single mother with little support? Do you want to be self-employed or start a business? Are you still trying to decide the type of business to choose, or do you have any prior business experience? You might want to purchase your first home but need more savings.

Consider your dream, then list all the details that have to do with it. A goal, ambition, or aspiration has lived in your core for as long as you can remember. Something that, when you finally achieve it, will transform you to the next level of yourself. Think about and concentrate on this one thing. Also, do not forget your social circle. Your network is also referred to as relationships. Who do you know who has more knowledge than you do and who you could contact to get assistance with this dream? Please be reminded that this process is a journey, not a destination, and quick answers are not expected.

What is the main obstacle that's keeping you from pursuing your dream?

The answer to this question can be a rabbit hole. The possibilities are endless. However, I encourage you to list every excuse you can think of for not pursuing your lofty goals. People who don't support you, money, worries, and other factors could be among them. There are numerous types of obstacles that you can thoughtfully remove.

Your dreams might not seem possible or realistic to some, or you could be afraid that others would mock you. You could not even be talented or skillful, in your opinion. All this negative self-talk could act as obstacles that prevent you from progressing. But only you have the final word should you choose to pursue it.

Once again, if you look for things that will stop you from taking a step, you will undoubtedly find them. So be very careful in this step, and don't be discouraged.

What passion are you hesitant to acknowledge or own?

Many people have aspirations and passions that they are reluctant to discuss for fear of ridicule from others. But unfortunately, we all have control of our narrative, and since we are the ones taking the journey, we are in the driver's seat. This is for you. It's time to let go of what others think.

This passion might be too wishful or unrealistic. But what is it? What did you aspire to be the most as a child? When you were younger, did you have dreams of becoming someone, but things didn't go as planned? Do you ever consider how your life may have changed if you had pursued your aspirations when you were younger? Would you follow this desire right now, given a chance?

What is the one thing you'll regret if today was your last day on Earth?

In a person's last few hours of life, many may experience remorse. Many people find it too late to make up for wasted opportunities. When they understand they are going to pass away soon, many people feel regret.

But unfortunately, it is frequently too late for many individuals to make up for wasted opportunities. If given a choice, they would have had utterly different lives. They would have lived differently if they had the chance to do it.

What would be your most significant regrets if a doctor informed you that you only had a few weeks to live? If you had more time left, what would you want to accomplish? There is no day but today to take the first step in your thousand-mile journey. Challenge yourself even if it's uncomfortable. Keep sight of where you'd want to go.

After responding to these questions, I hope you now have a clearer understanding of some of the things that bring you happiness and some of the dreams that have never left you. First, knowing what you've always wanted to do is essential. Second, imagine what you would buy if you won the lotto and how much money you would have. Then, how would you use yourself?

It's crucial to know these things. We play these dreams in our heads a million times in our lifetimes, but when you finally hit that jackpot, you don't ever want to forget those dreams. When you finally land your dream job, you want to remember how you got there and why you wanted to be there in the first place.

Four

It's Okay to Be Uncomfortable

"Spark of activation" is a phrase I love. These may be subtle reminders or "a-ha" moments that finally nudge you to take the next step. We all have innate abilities, which are crucial when considering how to take our dreams and turn them into reality.

There is always a window of opportunity to activate when you see that spark. Otherwise, you might lose the momentum to take the next step finally. It's as if you almost need to be on guard for when your best moments and strengths come to mind reminding you that you have accomplished things before so that you can use them to help you realize your dreams.

Just like an athlete, it takes practice. A jeweler polishes a gem to give it its absolute luster. Likewise, entering the door to achieve your goal will take determination, courage, stamina, and fortitude. Therefore, you must identify that spark that activates you, and take the following steps, even if they're uncomfortable, so you never lose momentum. It will give you the self-assurance you need to succeed.

The high points in your life are among your most remarkable

experiences. Again, no prior recognition is necessary. Your most memorable moments in life are those that started uncomfortable or too risky and ended up leaving you with a sense of high and pure joy.

What are some things you've loved and wished you could do again? Look at a few of your successes. When you were younger, you might have constructed a miniature house. You may have performed in front of an audience or played the piano wonderfully.

You can also use your current skills to aid in accomplishing your dreams. For example, organizing or marketing skills, if that's your expertise. In addition, there are likely talents you possess that you aren't even aware of. These talents may be in baking, gardening, talking to people and encouraging them, counseling, physical fitness, and more.

You can be more skilled in your field. You can be knowledgeable about a subject you find highly enjoyable. Think of it this way. You may enjoy reading about a topic that interests you. It turns out to be something that ignites the spark and reveals your secret passion. Consider an issue you are entirely informed about by choice rather than an obligation to your job. Writing a book about something you've become good at may help others, such as crocheting, woodworking, public speaking, etc.

A person's passion is sometimes an incidental discovery. The genuine passion you had years ago may have been a part of some of the best moments of your life. Remember when you used to run and always dreamed of winning the New York City Marathon? You might have written that dream off years ago if you now smoke. But you can still get in shape again and attempt your big goal. These steps can be transformational as well as healing.

As they say, it's not a job if you enjoy doing something. It would be best if you found the motivation to be excited and inspired. That's why going back and reflecting on your past to identify these spectacular moments is worth doing because these life highlights are like hidden treasures that, when found again, will continue to "wow" you as if they just happened again today.

I encourage you to pause for a moment and reflect. At one point in your life, you already did that one fantastic thing successfully, and you can do it again with renewed passion and commitment. We can never forget these moments that once gave us so much joy and inspiration.

Five

There's So Much to Discover

Curiosity, the foundation of passion, is one very significant thing. Curiosity leads to constant questioning and the search for solutions. Most of the time, they keep our minds engaged. The reason gets more robust when exercised, and you are intrigued. Like a large muscle, your brain may be strengthened by exercising it.

The genuine passion you wish you gained back is something that has the most potential to change your life. If not for inquisitive or people who question, society would not have seen progress. Curious people push the bounds that bring home the discovery of a lifetime. They challenge the status quo and think outside the box for other possibilities.

As they say, if you think of things that could go wrong, you'll always find them. There will always be a reason why we can't think outside the box, ask a probing question, do the right thing, or make an important decision. One thing is common underneath it all, and we all know it, fear!

This valid feeling can paralyze us from experiencing so much good in this world and great experiences at our fingertips. Cliche as it sounds, only you can hold yourself back. However, there are steps that you can take, little by little, to establish good habits.

Mind Positivism

Do I need to say more? The answer is no, but I'll continue anyway. Negative situations in life are still present, even if you choose to think positively. Positive thinking entails adopting a more constructive and positive outlook when dealing with unfavorable conditions. Instead of expecting the worst, you believe the best will occur.

Self-talk is frequently where constructive thought begins. The constant, silent dialogue that goes through your head is self-talk. There are both positive and negative automatic thoughts. You use logic and reason to some extent when you communicate with yourself. Other self-talk could result from expectations because of previous notions about what might happen or misconceptions you make because of ignorance.

Thinking positively is a skill that you can enhance. Even though the steps are straightforward, developing a new habit requires patience and practice. A pivotal guideline to follow at first is to refrain from saying anything to oneself that you wouldn't say to another person. Instead, be gentle and helpful to yourself. If you have a false belief, examine it logically and disprove it by emphasizing the positive traits.

Think about everything you must be thankful for. Then, during trying moments, give yourself permission to smile or chuckle. Look for the humor in mundane events. Life is more enjoyable when you can laugh about it.

If you wish to have a more optimistic outlook on life, figure out what needs to be improved. It would be best to determine the aspects of your life that you typically think adversely about. These can be related to work, your commute, life changes, or a relationship if you want to be more optimistic and think more positively. Start small by concentrating on one topic to address more constructively.

New Ideas are Opportunities

Eagerness to learn also allows you to see how things can be from different angles. When you are set in one way, items are limited because your mind is unwilling to accept another solution. It is much like your life. If you don't see your life becoming any more successful than it already is, then you won't be. If you can open your eyes to new ideas about how things can be, you are more willing to try them.

Curiosity is magical because it allows you to recognize and not just dismiss thoughts when they come to mind. When interested in something, you have a more open mind to receive new ideas. Thus, you minimize missing out on the crucial ones.

You must also be receptive to suggestions. Do not avoid the frequently expressed opinions you may disagree about. If others share the same, it may be worth contemplating and weighing the validity. You'll never know that one opinion that would have made a difference in your current life situation if you shut it down entirely in the beginning. Instead, allow yourself to ask additional questions, test alternative solutions, and welcome suggestions.

Be Receptive to New Opportunities

You'll be able to see a much different picture in almost any circumstance when your thinking is open to fresh ideas. As a result of your curiosity, your world will be wide open to new horizons and opportunities. These fantastic things we see and benefit from wouldn't be present the way they are now in an ordinary world if not for open-minded people.

The capacity to look past daily routines and uncover hidden aspects of life requires a very inquisitive mind. You have the power to create these universes and possibilities. The inquiring mind is entirely within your control.

Imagine this. You're more likely to stay motivated in your job and keep your group or company one step ahead of the competition if you're open to new ideas and have a creative mind. Of course, in every situation, you should bring a set of presumptions with you. Though many may prove accurate, putting your preconceptions to the test may lead to intriguing new possibilities.

Have you thought about home projects like expanding your home office? You know it would be a good investment, but you decide against going forward with the plan because you believe you cannot afford it. Don't accept that premise! Could you sell some other assets to raise money even though you might not have the funds right now? Could you work additional hours to pay back a loan that you took out? You would be amazed at how resourceful you could get if you fully believed in your actions.

Excitement

It's doubtful that you are even remotely intrigued if you are bored with your life. As a result of your wanting to observe things, curiosity creates excitement in your life. You'll constantly be drawn to new things, and there are tons of toys and technology that you like as well.

It's so much fun to spice up your life with adventure when you're naturally adventurous and curious. But, of course, you can still do whatever it is that you do routinely. However, this implies that you should also pay slightly closer attention to what is happening in your immediate surroundings than usual.

Even just mere preparation to go out to the store can be exciting. Don't forget the topic of seizing opportunities, no matter how small or insignificant they may look. The choice is yours to derive excitement while doing it. Learn how to use anticipation to make things exciting. What are your other options?

Developing Curiosity

You must get out of the routine of doing the same thing daily. Instead, you can cultivate curiosity to make yourself an exciting person and see the possibilities for your life. You are more likely to pursue your passions if you start to grow intrigued and genuinely want to know what your life will be like when you follow your dreams.

We already know that the most pleasing thing to do when cultivating your curiosity is to keep a flexible mind. Forgive me if I sound like a broken record but opening your mind can be the most challenging thing if you're stuck with your old habits. So when cultivating your curiosity, you should also avoid taking anything for granted.

Many individuals accept things as they are, while some always delve further and retain all excitement and interest. Even if it may seem simple, opportunities may come less frequently. Understanding the value of any chance to change your life will raise your appreciation of them.

These simple things occur so much that we tend not to pay as much significance to them as they serve. Think about the time you got your first job offer, a trip with a friend, and time with grandma. These moments are critical since you never know when they'll come again. Savoring these opportunities by converting them into unforgettable moments should force you to ask for more of these opportunities.

Ask questions every day to continue refining your interest. What others think of you is irrelevant. Being curious is necessary while you are working on yourself. You can do this to explore what's going on below the surface. Along with exercising your brain, learning new information and gaining knowledge are two other benefits.

You may find answers to why you react to certain situations as you learn about yourself. For example, even though you might accomplish something one way, others might decide to do it another way. Therefore, not everything should be done the same just because you've done it that way forever.

Do you pre-label things as enjoyable or bland? Don't prejudge activities because you had a terrible time doing them or were with someone who ruined your experience. You should get up and start doing something with someone else, even if it sounds boring. However, the only time something is dull is when you make it boring. When something is dismissed as flat, it effectively shuts the door on the possibility of it becoming fun.

Be spontaneous and creative; seize these moments and make them yours. Consider learning to be enjoyable. There are still a lot of things you need to understand about your passion. It's typical for people to believe they lack power because they cannot learn new things or consider themselves too old to imagine or discover. How heartbreaking is that?

You can always learn new things, no matter your age. You are a lifelong student constantly learning new things in the university called life. Another technique to satisfy and expand your interest is to read new stuff. Even if you like to concentrate on a single subject, you should read widely and be open to various topics. You may become even more curious because of this. If you don't like reading, audiobooks are available on demand. Again, no more excuses.

Therefore, approach your curiosity with a new attitude of excitement and fun. If you must take a class or read a book to learn something new, do it. You will know much more than if you thought learning was a chore.

Adding Imagination

Do you consider yourself to be lacking in creativity? Or you can think you're creative when you're not at all. Creativity is necessary to pursue your simple hobbies and turn them into action. I mean, if we cannot even accomplish the simpler things, wouldn't that raise a challenge for the bigger ones? You'll need to overcome obstacles in a variety of methods using creativity. You'll be more successful in life if you have more imagination. Here are a few strategies to help you develop creativity in your life.

In whatever you do, make creativity a game. You should set guidelines for yourself when you encounter a situation. Consider the goals and any potential roadblocks or strategic limitations. The more inventive you can be with these responses, the more efficient you become.

Setting goals is a necessary part of creativity. Goals require deadlines. Thus, you must set a time frame for your efforts. Tasks have more grit when they have a deadline attached to them. Additionally, you won't put things off as much.

Another crucial factor is self-expression. To express oneself as creatively as possible, you must grab every chance. Not only creatively but also at every opportunity. In seeking out ways to express yourself, you are being creative.

For example, presenting your meal on the plate is one way to express yourself. With garnishes and other additions, you could choose to spruce up the dish. Another example is that it's possible to radically alter how you deliver presentations at work that is different from how your company does it. Every action should be seen as a chance to be creative and a novel expression of your uniqueness.

Increase your level of focus. Keeping noise and distractions out of the way while you concentrate is one of the best things you can do while your creativity is in action. You will see opportunities and increased quality in your work product when you give it your full attention.

Something can only be uninteresting if you choose not to pay attention to it. Attempt to make it exciting once more. You should consider your tasks as smaller pieces of a larger image, primarily when you are engaged in tasks that appear monotonous. It would help if you looked at everything as its whole while placing the same importance on all its parts.

Explore Your Home More

A vital point of this book is understanding that your genuine passion can be there before you, but you may have trouble identifying it. I may have said it a few times, but it's worth revisiting. For example, you might amass collections of miniature items, books, hobbies that you like on the weekends, and more.

See if any of the decorations in your house hint at your genuine passion by taking a closer look. You could be shocked to discover that you've surrounded yourself with things that have been speaking to you without realizing it. Walking around the home can also trigger memories that bring you to a state of nostalgia.

I remember a day when I walked around the house and saw an old picture of my mom and me in 2009, a few months before she passed away. It made me realize that time passes and we only live once. That experience, and a few more, ignited my spark to get activated to write a book.

Six

When the Going Gets Tough

Many people are extremely clear about their passion. Yet, there are obstacles outside of themselves that prevent them from pursuing it. It helps you overcome any barriers preventing you from realizing your dreams. External obstacles are entirely under your control, and you can take action to overcome them. Our minds are flooded with fear and uncertainty when difficult times strike in life. In response to these emotions, our bodies exhibit physical symptoms of anxiety, such as a heaviness in the pit of the stomach, racing heartbeats, and gasping for air.

We are naturally restless and idle because of our physical makeup. Recognize that this is a normal reaction. You can decide whether to overcome difficult circumstances or to be destroyed by them. Your burning coal of "will-power" backed choice will produce enough steam (enthusiasm & new ideas) to propel your efforts toward success. It would help if you consciously exercised this direction of your mental muscles. The challenges will soon become smaller, dimmer, and invisible no matter how large they initially appear if you proceed in this manner.

What About Others?

Sometimes, consideration for the needs of others is a significant obstacle to someone from pursuing their passion and aspirations. The "I don't want to hurt or offend anyone" mentality is more rampant than we can ever imagine. But if we think like this all the time, we're not giving ourselves enough priority. We all know that we can't please everyone. So if you act in good faith and relatively every time, you've discharged your duty to humanity.

We usually hear commentary that is difficult to listen to since it makes you feel mocked. Your concept might sound unoriginal, considered ridiculous, and many other things. If an unfavorable outside view is given to you, you should listen to it last but with a grain of salt. This is okay, as you also need to guard your morale. You'll know when the right time is if at all, to examine these comments.

You need to surround yourself with encouraging people if you have a passion that you're willing to share. These people must be deserving of hearing about it. Plain and simple. You don't want to be around somebody who isn't encouraging since they will make you feel bad, but only if you permit them.

Many people find that their partner does not share their passions because they think they are absurd or because they would feel embarrassed to know what they are. But these reactions are sometimes because of their partners' lack of understanding and ignorance. Sometimes, in the absence of knowledge, people tend to speculate, which isn't always good. Your choices are limited if you prioritize your partner over your passion. Make sure your partner understands that you have a strong passion for something and that they must support you.

With the appropriate assistance, anything is possible. However, things might become challenging when family members are not emotionally supportive of one another. The best next step is to let them know you are following your aspirations. Whether they support you or not should not inhibit you from continuing your plans but putting them on notice shifts a level of responsibility to them to consider what you're working on in the decisions they make or things they say. Your life is yours. Until they see that it makes you happy, you might have to isolate yourself from those who aren't encouraging rather than stop taking action.

Financial Resources

Money is the root cause that keeps people from pursuing their passions. As an example, you might be a capable mechanic who has always wanted to open your own business but has put off the necessary preparations because of the cost. However, you can obtain quick cash. There are many ways to save money to start a business or engage in an expensive hobby. However, creating cutting costs in areas of your life where they are unnecessary is the best thing you can do.

A way you can save money in your life is by considering all your current unnecessary extra spending. Prominent practices include eating out for lunch every day at work. Instead, consider packing lunch. This is basic, I know, but we all need a reminder. Instead of driving to work daily, consider taking the bus, subway, or even walking on certain days to save money and exercise. You can buy many unnecessary items because you always shop for groceries when you're hungry rather than when you're not. They all add up, so don't be surprised.

Your creativity will aid in finding additional sources of income that you can set aside for your project. There may be a way to launch your dream without paying anything upfront. There are several options to launch your own business from home. If you love making cupcakes and want to own your shop, you can start your online business first. Nevertheless, your online business success is as significant as being successful with a brick-and-mortar store. If your partner is supportive, it will ease the financial burden while starting and allow you to pursue your goals.

Time

Another reason why many people don't follow their passions is that they say they don't have the time. This excuse is accurate if you commute a long distance to work, get home late at night, and have children to look after. In addition, many people frequently experience job burnout and never have time to spend with their families. So, when someone wants to take time off to pursue a passion, they feel guilty for putting themselves front and center.

You must devise a way to accomplish your goals if you require more time. Think about going to bed a little later or waking up earlier each day. Remember that sleep is essential for happiness and a good day, so you can only slightly reduce your sleep time.

You might be permitted to bring your laptop or crafts to work during your lunch break. Many of us work from home, so use your breaks to do something enjoyable. You can devote an hour each day to pursuing your passion. Finding the time is significant.

People frequently gripe about wasting time when they assert they don't have the time to pursue their passions. You might spend hours watching television every night and only get anything done on the weekends. Given your week of work, this might be an excellent time to unwind. Remember that happiness and a good day depend on getting enough sleep.

Assess the time you spend watching TV or hanging out with your pals. You can never be too restrictive, but balance is critical. You'll discover how much time you have to do things that equally matter, if not more.

You still have time to start. Enhance your time management skills. Remember that you make the rules when doing a personal project based on the priority you attached to it. If your project takes hours and you have an extra hour each day, you can work on it in segments. Then tackle pleasure in anticipation of resuming the work.

Employment

If your current job is why you cannot live out your passions because you are a slave to your employer, then you should find a new employer. I know. It sounds hasty and easier said than done. But honestly, what would you expect from spending more time doing that job? If you are not doing what you love to do in the first place, it won't matter if you find another employer.

Most people are thinking about their jobs differently due to the pandemic, which has unnerved them. You may have heard of the "Great Resignation," and many people leave their jobs. However, people are getting creative and have launched a "Great Rethink," which, in my opinion, is a movement.

The "Great Rethink" is a way to adapt and think creatively to address social or personal issues. This entails asking questions such as: Do you enjoy the culture at your workplace? Are you given the opportunities you want for advancement, and do you believe you are treated fairly? But, of course, the most crucial question is whether our work feels as meaningful to us as it should. If you answered in the negative to any of these questions, pause. There are some methods that people can use to increase the meaning of their lives and careers. These methods have come up through research into "deep purpose" organizations that care enough about employee well-being, engagement, and retention.

After launching this "Great Rethink" for yourself, determine if you can find what you're looking for elsewhere. But you should first be aware of your purpose. Attempt job creation if you do have that option. Try job crafting to ensure your responsibilities are consistent with this objective.

It would be best if you also considered your employer and boss to ensure they can support you in this endeavor. The time may have come to think about moving on if, despite your best efforts, you still need help understanding its significance. Even though you may depend on your job for a living, you should strive to live a happy and fulfilling life. You will only be successful if your job is the only thing that makes you happy.

You won't get ahead if you're in a job you detest. It might be a struggle to get out of bed and work daily. On the other hand, don't you desire a career that makes you eager to wake up each morning? This is entirely under your control, and you have the go-signal to make that choice.

Fears

We talked about fear so many times in this book. The reason is that fear is intertwined in many facets of our existence. Fear is one of the main obstacles keeping people from pursuing their passions and realizing their full potential. Of course, you must overcome your fears, but you can do it. Through the force of curiosity, you'll be more receptive to ideas and aware that there may be more options available than what your mind has led you to believe.

An article in Psychology Today mentioned that without fear, people wouldn't be able to defend themselves against real dangers. Throughout human evolution, fear has critically reacted to emotional and physical threats. In ancient times, this was crucial when both men and women faced life-or-death situations for basic human needs, like hunting or safety. These are still relevant issues, albeit repurposed to fit modern times.

Your fear of failure may be why you have yet to find that spark to ignite your passion into action. Failure is a word we also discussed in this book because it's common to be afraid of it. You could think about the time you were trying to learn to ride a bike or learn to swim. Someone often starts something new, pursues a passion, and succeeds immediately. Others may fail even before starting. There may be many worries and obstacles you run into along the way. Nevertheless, you must stand back up and carry on.

Fear of failure is understandable, but it shouldn't keep you from trying. You must view failure as an opportunity to help you move on and learn from it. Even achieving success can make you nervous. Despite the absurdity of it, many people are terrified of success. This pressure causes many people to struggle to earn and save money; when they do, some spend it on things they don't even need before they can pursue their goals. They later regret what they did and start the saving process over.

Never allow fear to hold you back from success. Because so many people don't believe they can succeed due to their low self-esteem, it is understandable that they experience anxiety. However, if you genuinely believe it, setting your mind to take you somewhere good will get you there.

We are All Lifelong Learners

Lifelong learning, as I discussed earlier, means just that. We stop learning when we die. We can only hope we leave a legacy full of lessons that continue to inspire those we leave behind. Even though it seems crucial, most people do not find lifelong learning necessary for their everyday lives. Most believe working more, socializing, or engaging in entertainment will yield far greater returns than looking at what they think are pointless materials. Sadly, most people also believe that lifelong learning is something they are obligated to do. Sounds senseless? We don't know what we don't know.

Learning presents a problem for many people as well. You may have decided that you are no longer interested in learning new things because of a 20-year-old education. On the other hand, you can always learn something new, even when you're 80 years old and in the final chapters of your life. The entire learning process must be viewed as exciting and enjoyable. Discovering new things should be exciting because you're growing physically and aging but a lot more knowledgeable.

Life is an obstacle course, and your dreams, visions, or goals are always behind these obstacles. Thus, leaving you no option but to do your best to overcome them. But, without knowledge, how do you suppose to overcome these obstacles? Whether applying conceptual or experiential learning, your chances of surviving the challenge are higher. Don't you agree? Once again, this choice is yours, and the prize behind the obstacle is for your taking.

Learning can be a roadblock if you allow it. Even if it's true to you, these are only temporary roadblocks. However, it is easy to use them as an excuse to remain where you are. You can influence how you think and remove obstacles from a lack of knowledge or experience. Whether or not the people in your life are helping you, you should stand on your own because you can. You are smart enough to have control over your job or the ability to develop novel ways to raise money for your projects. Your passion needs to flourish, so you must remove the obstacles.

Seven

Visioning

Using your hopes for the future as a light source is all that visioning entails. Setting goals is a crucial component of visioning for many reasons. Setting goals encourages ambition, allows you to monitor your progress, and gives you something to anticipate. You must first set your goals, though, to achieve them. There are more steps available in the following two chapters.

I mentioned in the last chapter that one of the most effective things you can do when setting goals is to assign a deadline for each milestone. Choose a purpose or passion and give it a completion date. After deciding on a deadline, you'll divide your goal into several steps to complete it.

These are all significant steps. Setting milestone-based goals enable you to monitor your progress toward a goal. Consider creating a chart and related actions. You can then divide each stage into tasks and other requirements. Next, you can give each milestone a date depending on how long it takes you to reach it. These dates may be estimated so that you could be off by one or two days. On the other hand, you might surpass some benchmarks before others, which could aid in getting you back on track.

When utilizing the goal technique, you always look forward to something. After completing each goal, rewarding yourself is never a bad idea. It could be symbolic of many different things that can boost your morale. Or, as you get closer to reaching your goal, picture the reward in your mind. You are more likely to work on a task when you have a deadline for completing it rather than saying, "I'll finish it someday." The goal becomes more concrete when it has a deadline.

Your motivation to pursue the objective and make it a reality will increase as you come to understand your true passion. If you need to hone your skills, enroll in a few classes. These lessons will be part of the milestones and actions you take to get where you want to go. You will get closer as you complete and reach a goal for each one.

If your goals require actions that are challenging and require a lot of effort on your part, feel free to treat yourself. For instance, buy a bottle of wine, take the evening off, and celebrate your success. In some way, reward yourself for your efforts. You deserve it because you are deserving.

You must carefully plan any endeavor you take. To arrive at your destination, you must divide each objective into several steps. Because it will seem much simpler to get the plan, you will have to work harder. However, you also have a way to assess your progress toward realizing the life you've always wanted. Loving yourself is learning the quality of your steps in your journey and understanding that this is your journey and a rewarding one.

Eight

Your Passion in Action in Your Daily Life

Do you have too much zeal? Do you think it's terrible? It's comparable to claiming that the music or sugar is too loud. With passion comes a meaningful life. To you, what has meaning? Run each day? Meditation? Your occupation? Children? Pets of yours? Something you care deeply about? The essence of your motivation should be simple.

It's become standard career advice to "follow your passion." In analyzing the definition of "passion" in the workplace, we need to look at its root word considering its current usage. Passion symbolizes both intense sexual desire and self-sacrifice. Passion is the one word that captures the cycle of life, referring to both sex and death. Passion's Latin root, "pati," which means "to suffer," made it famous in Christian theology to describe the martyrs' self-sacrifice-inflicted suffering.

The word "passion" started to be used, in opposition to its original meaning, to express sexual love and a strong liking or enthusiasm in the sixteenth century. Even though The Passion of the Christ depicts pain and suffering, today's word "passion" is often associated with excitement.

Modernly, "passion" conjures up strong associations of pleasure and desire. However, it can still refer to pain and suffering, as seen in The Passion of the Christ.

Your passions may dictate changes in your life, including your attitude and lifestyle. Your commitment, vigor, and drive to realize your vision of success come from your passion for what you do. Deepak Chopra is the author of one of my favorite quotes, "Always follow your passions. Never question whether something is attainable or not. Continue your path, and don't let self-limiting thoughts stop you from pursuing your passion."

Success can be determined by any metric you choose. Being prosperous financially is optional for success. Suppose the aim of pursuing your passion is to achieve financial success; good for you. You are more likely to be successful in making money when you seek a goal that you are incredibly passionate about. Your ability to look back on your life and recognize your accomplishments is the most significant aspect because somewhere in your life, you believe in something that you can do, and it's worth exploring that.

Nine

You are What Makes You Whole

"Wholeness is our capacity to experience health as transcending all limitations while accepting them, overcoming this virus of perfectionism which keeps us locked into an imaginary world rather than the real world...it is paradoxically in accepting (limitations) that we can transcend them."— Laurence Freeman.

You can experience wholeness, so let's start there. Period. Health is "a state of total physical, mental, and social well-being and not merely the absence of disease or infirmity," according to the World Health Organization. We are very good at defining what is wrong with us in psychology and mental health, but what does it mean to be proper, healthy, or whole? If we were to see it, would we recognize it?

What does wholeness look like for you or me? Because it involves everything that makes us human—mind, body, soul, emotions, and relationships—wholeness is a complicated topic. None of these things can be dissected, examined under a microscope, or studied scientifically in a vacuum. You could say that we can analyze the body at the molecular level and dissect it, and you'd be correct. But does this provide accurate or comprehensive information about how the body interacts with the soul or emotions? I'm not so sure.

We all desire to feel complete. The reality is it is impossible to obtain. We frequently experience our brokenness more acutely the harder we work to heal. Realizing and accepting oneself as a "whole" is necessary. On wholeness, there is a wealth of additional information.

Furthermore, you can start experiencing it without the help of another person. Anyone who asks will receive it as a gift and without charge. This is because you already possess the ability to achieve it. However, you will quickly learn that it requires physical, emotional, mental, and even spiritual capital to accomplish a goal, work toward becoming a better version of yourself, or improve your life and relationships. Sometimes life can seem like a piece of cloth with holes where joy, faith, and hope slowly erode before we can truly embrace them. It will get harder to believe that becoming whole is a reality if you live long enough because moments will occur when you feel empty, lost, and incomplete.

But if you know how to look for or augment the missing parts using techniques and lessons learned in your journey to loving yourself, you'll continue to find pleasure in your lifelong journey to wholeness.

Be Enthusiastic

Some individuals are just irresistible. You can be at ease around them, and they never try very hard. These individuals have a zest for life. Are you considering joining that group? For more information on what makes an enthusiastic person and how to become one yourself, continue reading. You can make a minor deal about your passion for people to see. But you must be motivated internally, which will come naturally if you genuinely appreciate your actions. To be enthusiastic, you must be interested in and enjoy what you do. In other words, it means avoiding a passive attitude in favor of one that is motivated and active.

Enthusiasm is a positive outlook, a sense of fulfillment from accomplishing goals, and a drive to succeed. Making clay pots will make you passionate about the caliber of your output and proud of your work so that you won't provide a customer with a broken pot. Given your pride in this, you will be proud of whatever you do because it will be in your name and be your property, somewhat of your trademark.

Role Models

You love yourself enough to believe that pursuing your passion and taking action is possible. However, part of this natural process is for others to directly see what you're doing or because they've experienced it. This is an opportunity to demonstrate to others that achieving your goals is possible.

Leadership is another role where a select few can share this mindset of possibilities. The actions and personalities of role models serve as examples for others and motivate those around them to act. In addition, role models may inspire others to want to follow in their footsteps.

Leaders are role models through exemplary integrity, tenacity, optimism, and hope. Because they are respected and admired, role models silently attract followers as they display qualities and behaviors that they would like them to possess. Pick at least five people you want to be like if you want to succeed. Then, learn as much as you can about them. Find out what makes them successful.

Holding a formal leadership position is optional to set an example for others in your organization or field. Leadership can be demonstrated in your personal life or household. Your simple conduct and exemplary work ethic demonstrate your ability to lead by example for coworkers, your spouse, children, or the community.

I'm not suggesting that you try to imitate other leaders but using them as role models to develop your uniqueness as a leader-role model is powerful. Being a change agent in your life should ignite your passion. Living your life the way you want means changing significantly while also being able to carry the responsibility of inspiring others.

Improving Daily

You might not consistently achieve your best work while pursuing your passion. If processes slow you down, produce subpar work, or are frustrating, you must think outside the box. Remember this concept? This is an opportunity to practice creative thinking. You'll get better and realize how good you can be over time.

Productivity rises gradually after you learn how to make things better. However, when you first start pursuing your passion, everything might appear chaotic and out of order. You can solve this problem, but it will take some time and work. You may take fifteen attempts to find the most practical and successful method.

There is no difference, beginning with a choice of 1 point better or 1 percent worse. (In other words, it won't significantly affect you today.) But because these minor improvements or drops over time compound, the gap between those who consistently make better decisions and those who don't quickly widen. By the end of a year, if you improve by 1% daily, you will be 365 times better than when you started. Because of this, even seemingly insignificant decisions can significantly impact over time.

Taking the Next Steps

When you are living your passion in action, it must be all around you. You want to avoid running into the same issue again because it has been so simple to put off working toward your passion. Therefore, it would be best to surround yourself with people who can aid you. The key to avoiding procrastination is to act.

Your dream is a fundamental goal that you want to see. Hang a sign that says "action" to remind yourself that you are pursuing your passion through nonstop action. You want members of your team who are equally committed to acting. Avoid working together with people who lack initiative. Let's look at this scenario. You can only ask an encouraging aunt to help you pursue your passion if she would rather lounge around and chat than do hard work. She might be the one who can assist you in creating buzz about your endeavor or company without taking any action. Find a place for her to help; it would be best if you had assistance.

Keep up the excellent work. Always hold yourself accountable for setting goals and acting. You would like to thank everyone who has helped you. This gesture does not mean you must spend the money you don't have. To express gratitude, you can tell someone how much you appreciate their assistance. Sometimes acknowledging someone's actions is sufficient, especially if they know you value their efforts.

Ten

Loving Yourself Enough to Make Your Dreams A Reality

You have now arrived at the lessons learned from reading this book. You started by thinking about what loving yourself means and the many ways you can nurture yourself. Next, it's about treating yourself well and realizing that you deserve love and acknowledgment and have a rightful place in this world. This is followed by the practice of not letting your mistakes define who you are; instead, focus on what you can learn from them. Finally, being aware of and taking care of your daily and physical body's needs will keep you sustained and withstand challenges along the path.

Acknowledging Your Accomplishments

We are given a blank page to write on each day and a fresh slate on which to start new projects. And it's unquestionably a good idea to continue approaching our relationships and lives with a forward-looking mindset. It's important to give yourself breaks when you need them and to stop telling yourself that you aren't good enough when you are. But it's also beneficial to occasionally take a moment to reflect on our accomplishments. We don't want to dwell on the past, even when it is a good thing. Being present and concentrating on who we are becoming are essential components of living well.

Furthermore, nothing we have done in the past excuses us from our obligations. Whatever we accomplished yesterday, we must still turn up today and complete the task. Recognizing the distance we've traveled is helpful in tandem. When we feel like we are in a never-ending rat race, only able to see the next thing that needs to be done, it is more difficult to fight the urge to give in to despair. Justifying the good we've already accomplished and celebrating the difference we've made are both considered accomplishments.

Also, hating or blaming yourself for missed opportunities wastes time. That's accurate! The bottom line is that everything in our lives is time, season, and purpose. You are allowing passion for taking action today because your path and past experiences have prepared you for it. But you got here because you also recognized that the only way to achieve something is to love yourself enough to work on it. But now that you know how to find and follow your passion, which will eventually lead you to find joy in that area of your life, you must breathe life into it through simple steps that you can practice daily through positive affirmations.

Positive Affirmations

I now encourage you to use these affirmations to practice loving yourself and finding the joy you deserve. Positive statements called affirmations to serve to reinforce good attitudes and thoughts. The most effective way to say them is usually in front of a mirror. They are typically noted in the present tense first person (I, me, myself, etc.). If you find a phrase or sentence that resonates with you, precede it with an "I." It could be an excerpt from a book, poem, TEDx talk, etc. Positive affirmations are a vital component of "the law of attraction," which states that we can change our thoughts and mindset to attract good things into our lives. They do work and can do wonders for boosting our motivation and keeping our thoughts on the bright side.

It would be best to practice positive affirmations in the morning because your mind is becoming alert. If you're not careful, negative thoughts may enter your mind at this crucial time. For example, you may think that you're tired, that the weather is unpleasant, that you don't like your job or other limiting thoughts that may cause you to feel down. Therefore, focusing your thoughts and emotions on the positive in the morning is crucial, and positive affirmations can help you do that. These affirmations are mere recommendations, and you can develop your own that makes the most sense.

Believe

"If you believe in your dream with all your heart, you can achieve it." — Lailah Gifty Akita.

Loving yourself includes believing in your abilities. It entails having faith in your ability to carry out your commitments and trusting that your efforts will yield the desired results. Thus, believing in yourself stems from several significant psychological experiences. As mentioned in previous chapters, self-worth, self-acknowledgment, and self-trust are a few of these experiences.

Believing in your capacity to succeed is the essential element of success. Since your abilities are contained in your thoughts, you have total control over how successful you are. It's not a case of trying to convert them. You're not obligated to tell anyone about your belief.

Instead, remain calm and confident in your accomplishment. One day, you'll be excited to discuss your passion and how you turned it into a reality. Have confidence and a sense of empowerment as you consider your tasks and how you will succeed.

Changing Your Attitude

"I reject all negative feelings about myself and my life, and I consciously accept all that is good."—Anonymous.

You could succeed or fail based on your attitude. Therefore, you must keep your attitude entirely engaged and interested. Always keep a positive outlook. Don't allow trivial issues to depress or irritate you. You are pursuing your passion, and every challenge you face now is an opportunity to learn. Therefore, you must now have a positive attitude in all you do related to your business and your passion.

A positive attitude will make you more successful in your business and interest. You must have faith and an optimistic mindset. It depends on how you view it. The important thing is how you see something, not how horrible it is. There's a tendency for some who doubt themselves to wreak havoc on circumstances and things. Things will work more frequently than ever if you keep a level of optimism and glass "half-full" attitude.

Craft Your Plans

"I have the power and ability to create all the success and prosperity I desire."—Anonymous.

If you're in a situation where you can't make your passion a reality right now, you'll need to modify your goals. By focusing on the details of your execution, you can hone and improve your idea. Describe your project's strategy considering all relevant factors. You can do many things while you wait. When there is a waiting period, think of it as borrowed time or an additional opportunity to get better rather than a signal or an excuse to put off beginning something.

Maintaining the Momentum

"The universe is filled with endless opportunities for me, and I pursue them with purpose and vigor."—Anonymous.

Putting your ideas into action is the quickest way to gain momentum when pursuing your passion. Take your time with things to happen or come to you. Act now. The same is true for a problem you need to fix. If you did something, it would be beneficial. The more responsive you are, the more momentum you begin to build that is difficult to stop. Your productivity will increase as your sluggishness goes away.

Utilize Your Resources as Best You Can

"Feeling confident, secure, and strong is a normal part of my everyday life, and I have all that I need to make this a great day."—Anonymous.

You must utilize and optimize your available resources to maintain forward momentum. You might have little money, so you'll need to devise inventive ways to pay for things like daycare and errands. Friends and other people can lend a hand. If you're working on building something, ask if you can find more supplies if you are starting to run low. Be resourceful.

Smart people ask for assistance. When productive people are ignorant of something, they admit it. Asking for assistance rather than attempting to figure something out on your own saves time (and frustration). Make asking for help a habit and ensure you are aware of your resources.

Sacrifice and Hard Work

"We must be willing to let go of the life we planned to have, the life that is waiting for us,"—Joshua Campbell.

When someone pursues their passion, they are frequently prepared to put in a lot of work and make many sacrifices. When you start your new job, you might realize that you are initially cash-poor. To succeed later, you must plan. Although some things will take time, seek the joy of working while you wait. Any person who aspires to be at the top must put in a lot of effort. What is the expected amount of work?

You will need to exert more effort than other people if you want to be the best. In the off-season, Kobe Bryant averaged 2000 shots per day. Yet, he had the willingness to put in the necessary effort to excel.

While anyone can remain ordinary, those who put in the effort and go about daily will rise above the mundane and achieve extraordinary things. You'll have to work a lot of overtime, skip family time, and complete many other tasks. If you want to succeed, sacrifice is the most important thing you can do. This balancing can sometimes feel like another goal to sustain or a passion for pursuing. So be mindful of the signs that you're burning out.

There is no substitute for putting in the necessary effort to reach your goals. The only person who can help you achieve the goals you've set for yourself is you, and it will take action to reach the destination you seek. So accept the long days, tears, and sweat because they will pay off in the end.

Get Your Life in Order

"Make way for the unprecedented and watch your reality rearrange yourself," poet Yrsa Daley-Ward.

Plan your life around the inspiration that ignited you. For instance, let's say you've started a new business or a hobby that you hope will be successful. Start living the prosperous day you've always imagined after that. Get up early, for instance, and make coffee, read the newspaper, make your bed, blog, and other things. Optimize your time by setting it up effectively. Remind yourself of your visioning process. Then, make informed decisions and take care of your mind and body.

Implement the plans of practicing daily affirmations, meditations, and other exercises. You'll need to put in a lot of hours at first, but you can only succeed and increase your output by working hard for it. Eventually, you will perform these actions naturally and effortlessly. As a reminder, involve your loved ones in your plans and get their support because your success also becomes their success. Remember what I talked about earlier? Making 1% daily improvements will make you 365% better in a year. Every effort counts.

Eleven

The New You

Meet your new self. You've started to take center stage for the first time. You are reaping the rewards of being validated as good enough, deserving of love and acceptance, capable of being uncomfortable, and deserving of the joy of living authentically. You will now need to complete a few more tasks while living out your genuine passion.

You must save as much time and effort as possible for the spark that ignites you. The rest will happen naturally if you are committed and focused on your passion. When pursuing a passion, the pain and pleasure principle is irrelevant. It may please you since you enjoy doing it, making you happy to see the outcomes daily. Nevertheless, achieving your goals could be difficult and irritating. At times, you could cry and want to give up.

Success is never simple, but you would much prefer striving for your passion than a job you despise every day. You are the owner of this desire. Make the pain gratifying in every way by experiencing it. Your soul will be satisfied by the anguish, which is far better in the long run because you won't look back and regret anything.

Refrain from focusing on outcomes. The universe will manage results. In the beginning, progress could seem slow, and if all you focus on are the outcomes, you might never make it. Instead, according to Tao, find your path to freedom by concentrating on what you need to do.

When pursuing your passion, never worry about your survival. The secret to pursuing a passion is this. Worrying or being afraid will make your problems worse. Instead, believe that you will be okay and genuinely practice bravery because you can. You are capable. Everything is within your control, and positivity is within your reach. Most of all, always try to stay calm.

Twelve

The Final Thoughts: Are You Ready?

Loving yourself first is the key to unlocking endless possibilities in your life. The techniques described in the book offer concepts and viewpoints that can help motivate you to think creatively. For a moment, it encourages you to visualize a life filled with passion and joy as you work to achieve your goals.

You were born to do what you are passionate about, after all. Everyone has a passion. However, if you are clear on what it is and what steps to take to pursue it, you can use your passions to bring you lifelong joy. There are numerous methods for discovering your passion.

You can find your true passion by digging deeply within yourself and being honest to live authentically. The saying goes, "we may fool others, but we can't fool ourselves." If obstacles are in your path and you genuinely want something, you must get past them. If you have the willpower, you can do it.

For many people, there are many different ways to define success. Your definition of success is unique to you. Success is determined by what has the most personal meaning to you, not by things that can be seen or touched. Your objectives are, nonetheless, established so you can create an action plan to achieve them. Yes. You alone; nobody else.

You will inevitably encounter excuses, so develop the ability to push them aside one by one. Finally, celebrate your accomplishments as you pass significant checkpoints and progress toward your goals. This pat on the back is critical.

You are someone who merits pursuing your passion. The same things that anyone else can do are also possible for you. Never forget that you have filled your cup and are ready to act when you love yourself first. By learning to love yourself first, you have reclaimed your rightful place in this world as a deserving, whole person. You are seen and heard with many privileges and opportunities to find joy and do everyday things that make you happy.

You are enough. You are ready. It's time to ignite the spark that fires your soul!

"Your crown has been bought and paid for. Put it on your head and wear it!"—Maya Angelou.

Thirteen

Resources

16 Positive Affirmations for Believe in yourself. (2022, July 4). Find Motivation.https://findmotivation.org/believe-in-yourself-affirmations/

Academy, S. U. S. (2017, August 7). The road to success comes through hard work, determination, and personal sacrifice. The Sport Journal. https://thesportjournal.org/article/the-road-to-success-comes-through-hard-work/

Adults of Reddit, when you were younger did you have dreams and aspirations? If not where are you in life and how did you decide to get there? (2019, June 19). Reddit.
https://www.reddit.com/r/AskReddit/comments/c2e66w/adults_of_reddit_when_you_were_younger_did_you/

Borge, J. (2021, May 19). *40 Positive Affirmations to Add to Your Daily Rotation.* Oprah Daily.https://www.oprahdaily.com/life/relationships-love/g25629970/positive-affirmations/?slide=30

Carey, A. G. (2022, April 13). *Core Value Spotlight: Your Passion in Action.* Sendero
Consulting.
https://www.senderoconsulting.com/core-value-spotlight-your-passion-in-action/

Carlisle, C. (2022, August 20). *Acknowledging our accomplishments.* Dr. Corey Carlisle. https://coreycarlisle.org/acknowledging-our-accomplishments/

Doctorpedia. (2022, June 22). *The Differences Between Prayer and Meditation - Faith Article.* https://www.doctorpedia.com/channels/the-differences-between-prayer-and-meditation/

English, O. (2021, January 25). *Why loving yourself is the key to achieving your dreams!*
Oonagh English. https://www.oonaghenglish.com/articles/why-loving-yourself-is-the-key-to-
achieving-your-dreams

Enthusiastic People: Traits and Values. (2019, March 29). Exploring Your Mind.
https://exploringyourmind.com/enthusiastic-people-traits-values/

Ghenaiet, A. (2022, October 27). *Earn Extra Cash With These Side Hustles.* INK.
https://inkforall.com/ai-writing-tools/generate-startup-ideas/most-profitable-side-hustle/

Grover, J. (2021, October 12). What is Wholeness? Abundant Life Counseling. http://www.abundantlife-counseling.com/blog/2016/11/8/the-search-for-

wholeness

How to Help a Victim of Domestic Violence. (2022, August 29). Verywell Mind. https://www.verywellmind.com/how-to-help-a-victim-of-domestic-violence-66533

How to Master the Art of Continuous Improvement. (2022, August 31). James Clear. https://jamesclear.com/continuous-improvement

If Shawn & Ryan had the chance. (2022, August 25). Reddit. https://www.reddit.com/r/StreetOutlaws/comments/wwy7lj/if_shawn_ryan_had_the_chance/

Joy vs happiness: 3 ways to build a more joyful life. (2022, March 8). Psychologies. https://www.psychologies.co.uk/joy-vs-happiness/

Me., L. (2022, October 10). *A Short Guide to Becoming Whole: An Essential Part of Success*.Life Me. https://thelifemeblog.com/2014/01/11/becoming-whole/

Mind Tools. (2021, November 10). *New Ideas - Strategies and Techniques - Creativity Tools From MindTools.com*.https://www.mindtools.com/pages/article/newCT_88.htm

Owens, S. (2022, January 20). *5 Things You Must Do To Make Your Dreams Reality*. SummerOwens S.O. What! https://summerowens.com/5-things-you-must-do-to-make-your-dreams-reality/

Positive thinking: Stop negative self-talk to reduce stress. (2022, February 3). Mayo Clinic.https://www.mayoclinic.org/healthy-lifestyle/stress-management/in-depth/positivethinking/art20043950?reDate=28102022

Priority vs responsibilities for joint caregiving. Any advice? (2022, October 20). © 2007-2022 AgingCare All Rights Reserved. https://www.agingcare.com/questions/priority-vs-responsibilities-for-joint-caregiving-any-advice-477733.htm

Rose, S. (2018, March 9). *The Meaning of Passion.* https://www.linkedin.com/pulse/meaning-passion-steve-rose

S, S. (2020, March 4). *When the going gets tough, what do you do?*https://www.linkedin.com/pulse/when-going-gets-tough-what-do-you-samson-s

The Great Resignation or the Great Rethink? (2022, March 25). Harvard Business Review.https://hbr.org/2022/03/the-great-resignation-or-the-great-rethink

The University of Nottingham. (n.d.). *Entrepreneurship, Innovation and Management MSc –University of Nottingham.* Retrieved October 26, 2022, from https://www.nottingham.ac.uk/pgstudy/course/taught/entrepreneurship-innovation-and-management-msc

Thomas, G. (2020, December 2). *Surround Yourself With People Who Can Make You Grow And Stretch.* Leadership First.https://www.leadershipfirst.net/post/surround-yourself-with-people-who-can-make-you-grow-and-stretch-3

Want To Know What Your Life WIll Be Like In 10 Years? Then Pick Your Favorite New Among Us Mod! (n.d.). quiztest.me- Hot Test Real Me Quizzes. Retrieved October 26, 2022, from https://www.quiztest.me/en/test/4688.html?cat=Game

What is the healthiest way to eat? Here's the answer. (n.d.). Optum. Retrieved October 29, 2022, from https://www.optum.com/health-articles/article/healthy-living/what-healthy eating/?utm_source=PPC

What would you do if you had no choice but to bake a cake with a message that you take offense to? (2016, September 14). Reddit. https://www.reddit.com/r/AskReddit/comments/52pf1j/what_would_you_do_if_you_had_no_choice_but_to/

Yassine, N. (2019, December 27). *Do it because you are ENOUGH, Because you are worth it.* Boujeez Luxury Lifestyle & Fashion Magazine.deserve-it/https://www.boujeez.com/do-it-because-you-are-enough-because-you-are-worth-it-and-you-deserve-it/

Young, S. (2018, April 3). *The Goal of Learning Everything.* Scott H Young.https://www.scotthyoung.com/blog/2008/06/12/the-goal-of-learning-everything/

About the Author

Dr. Carl Carado holds a doctorate in education and a law degree, in addition to being a registered nurse. He also considers it an honor and a privilege to have served in the U.S. Army and U.S. Air Force. As a teen, he struggled with his sexuality and dealt with societal and family acceptance issues as an adult. As a result, he endured emotional, physical, and psychological abuse, depression, and shame. Dr. Carl has dedicated many years to figuring out his place in society while navigating internal conflicts related to faith, race, relationships, and self-acceptance. His passion for helping others get to a place of self-acceptance is now his lifelong journey. Today, he shares that our most incredible armor is accepting our true selves wholeheartedly and living our authentic lives fearlessly.

CPSIA information can be obtained
at www.ICGtesting.com
Printed in the USA
LVHW070512301122
734192LV00021B/1061

9 781959 928003